North American
INDIAN NATIONS

NATIVE PEOPLES
of the
PLATEAU

Krystyna Poray Goddu

LERNER PUBLICATIONS • MINNEAPOLIS

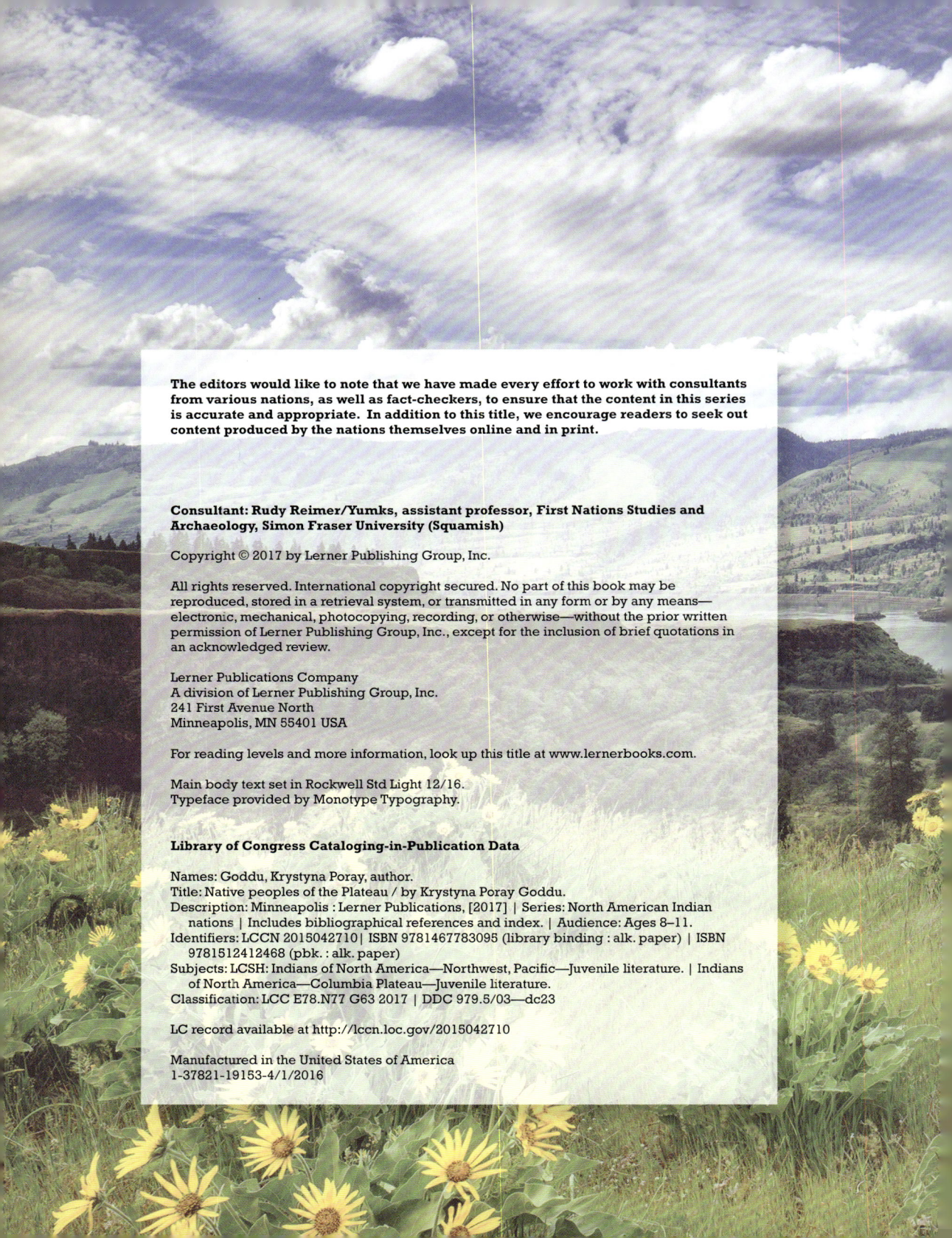

The editors would like to note that we have made every effort to work with consultants from various nations, as well as fact-checkers, to ensure that the content in this series is accurate and appropriate. In addition to this title, we encourage readers to seek out content produced by the nations themselves online and in print.

Consultant: Rudy Reimer/Yumks, assistant professor, First Nations Studies and Archaeology, Simon Fraser University (Squamish)

Copyright © 2017 by Lerner Publishing Group, Inc.

All rights reserved. International copyright secured. No part of this book may be reproduced, stored in a retrieval system, or transmitted in any form or by any means—electronic, mechanical, photocopying, recording, or otherwise—without the prior written permission of Lerner Publishing Group, Inc., except for the inclusion of brief quotations in an acknowledged review.

Lerner Publications Company
A division of Lerner Publishing Group, Inc.
241 First Avenue North
Minneapolis, MN 55401 USA

For reading levels and more information, look up this title at www.lernerbooks.com.

Main body text set in Rockwell Std Light 12/16.
Typeface provided by Monotype Typography.

Library of Congress Cataloging-in-Publication Data

Names: Goddu, Krystyna Poray, author.
Title: Native peoples of the Plateau / by Krystyna Poray Goddu.
Description: Minneapolis : Lerner Publications, [2017] | Series: North American Indian nations | Includes bibliographical references and index. | Audience: Ages 8–11.
Identifiers: LCCN 2015042710 | ISBN 9781467783095 (library binding : alk. paper) | ISBN 9781512412468 (pbk. : alk. paper)
Subjects: LCSH: Indians of North America—Northwest, Pacific—Juvenile literature. | Indians of North America—Columbia Plateau—Juvenile literature.
Classification: LCC E78.N77 G63 2017 | DDC 979.5/03—dc23

LC record available at http://lccn.loc.gov/2015042710

Manufactured in the United States of America
1-37821-19153-4/1/2016

CONTENTS

INTRODUCTION — 5

CHAPTER 1
LIVING OFF THE LAND — 10

CHAPTER 2
SOCIETY AND CEREMONY — 18

CHAPTER 3
FUNCTIONAL ART — 24

CHAPTER 4
FACING CHANGE — 30

CHAPTER 5
A THRIVING LAND AND CULTURE — 36

NOTABLE PLATEAU INDIANS — 42
TIMELINE — 43
GLOSSARY — 44
SELECTED BIBLIOGRAPHY — 45
FURTHER INFORMATION — 45
INDEX — 47

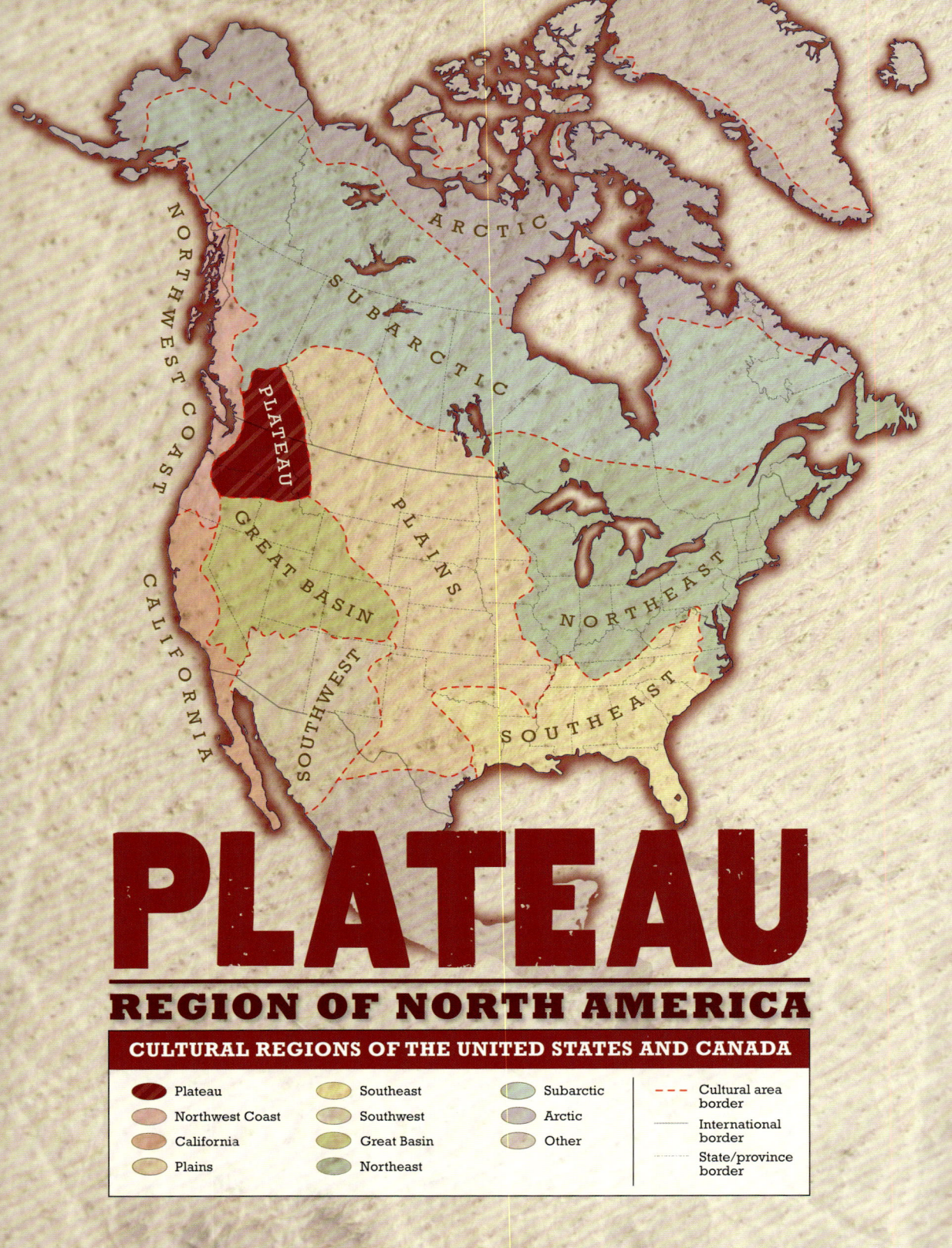

INTRODUCTION

Coyote was angry because a giant monster had eaten all of his friends. He decided to stop the monster and told the monster to eat him too. When the monster had eaten him, Coyote found all the other animals safe inside the monster. Coyote started a fire inside the monster's belly. The monster died, and all the animals escaped.

To celebrate, Coyote decided to create a new creature—humans. Coyote cut the monster into four pieces and threw the pieces to the north, south, east, and west. Where the pieces landed, humans came to be. Finally, Coyote washed the monster's blood from his hands. The drops of blood created more people.

This is one of many stories describing how the Plateau Indians came to live in the Columbia River plateau. This area is a flat, raised surface of land—a plateau—surrounded by the Rocky Mountains, Canadian Coast Mountains, and Cascade Range. The region covers parts of Canada and the United States, including British Columbia, Montana, Idaho, Washington, Oregon, and California. It is filled with lakes, rivers, and trees.

The Plateau Indians who live in this area descended from people who spoke languages from several language families.

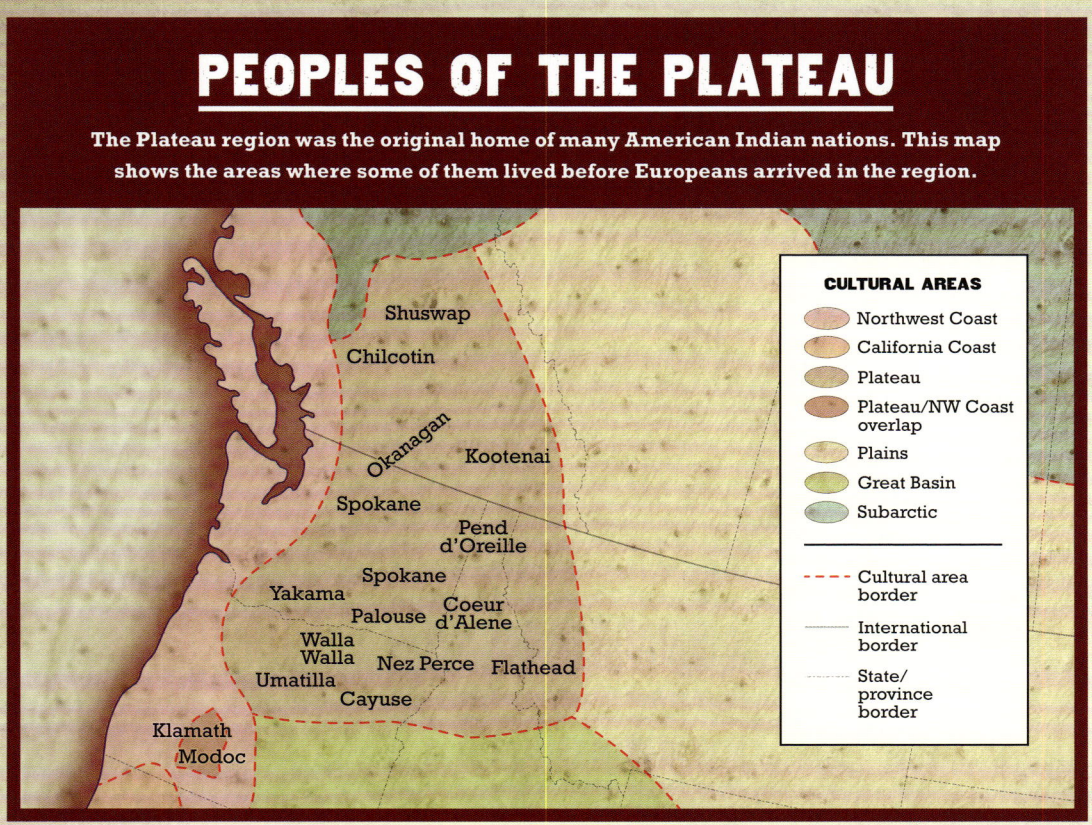

PEOPLES OF THE PLATEAU

The Plateau region was the original home of many American Indian nations. This map shows the areas where some of them lived before Europeans arrived in the region.

These families included Dene (DEN-ay), Salishan (SAY-li-shen), Sahaptin (sah-HAP-tyn), Kootenai (KOOT-un-nay), and Klamath-Modoc (KLAM-uth MO-dock).

There are several well-known Plateau nations. The Nez Perce (nes-PURSE), Cayuse (ky-YOOS), Palouse (puh-LOOS), Umatilla (Yoo-ma-TILL-a), Walla Walla (WOL-uh WOL-uh), and Yakama (YAK-uh-muh) lived on the Northern Plateau. The Pend d'Oreille (Pon-duh-RAY)—also known as the Kalispel (KAL-uh-spell)—Coeur d'Alene (kur-duh-LANE), Flathead, and Spokane (spo-KAN) lived on the Interior Plateau. The Klamath and Modoc lived in the southernmost region of the Plateau. The Kootenai lived in a region covering parts of British Columbia, Idaho, and Montana.

Along with the Kootenai, British Columbia was also home to several other nations, including the Shuswap (SHUH-shwahp), Okanagan (OH-keh-nah-gan), and Chilcotin (chil-COH-tin).

The Plateau peoples were surrounded by the native peoples of the Subarctic, the Northwest Coast, California, the Plains, and the Great Basin. Each of those cultures influenced the Plateau Indians. The southern part of the Plateau overlaps with the northern part of the Great Basin. So the cultures of the

LANGUAGE FAMILIES OF THE PLATEAU NATIONS

LANGUAGE FAMILY	MAJOR PEOPLES
Klamath-Modoc	Modoc, Klamath
Kootenai	Kootenai
Sahaptin	Nez Perce, Cayuse, Palouse, Yakama, Walla Walla, and Umatilla
Salishan	Spokane, Pend d'Oreille, Coeur d'Alene, Flathead, Shuswap, and Okanagan.
Dene	Chilcotin

nations in this overlapping area are similar. Plateau peoples met the Plains Indians around the eighteenth century. Many of the Plateau nations began following the practices of the Plains Indians. These practices included using leather for clothing, horse saddles, and bridles.

During the nineteenth century, Euro-American explorers, fur traders, and missionaries came to the Plateau. They brought unrest, violence, and disease to the Plateau nations. By 1850, the

The Columbia River was important to the livelihood of many Plateau nations.

population had been cut in half. In the nineteenth and twentieth centuries, the US government passed laws and made policies that took land and traditions away from the Plateau peoples. Many nations were moved to small areas of land called reservations. Some fought against becoming part of Euro-American culture. But in the end, all the Plateau peoples had to leave behind many of their traditional ways of life. The Plateau peoples weren't able to get back some of their lands and rights until the late twentieth century. Many are still working to protect the region of their ancestors and to give new life to their cultures.

A Flathead woman

CHAPTER 1
LIVING OFF THE LAND

The Plateau Indians gathered wild plants to eat, such as bitterroot.

The Plateau Indians were seminomadic. In the winters, they settled in permanent villages of a few hundred to a few thousand people. Usually these villages were near a river or stream. In warm weather, the people traveled between these villages and camps that were bases for hunting, gathering, and fishing.

Food

Fishing was the main source of food for most Plateau nations. Salmon was an important food for those who lived along the Columbia River, such as the Nez Perce, the Yakama, and

This Nez Perce man uses a long harpoon to spear salmon from a river.

the Umatilla. These peoples caught the fish from riverbanks or canoes. Their canoes were made from bark or hollowed-out logs. The Plateau Indians speared the salmon with harpoons or caught them in baskets that they hung near waterfalls. Sometimes they even used their bare hands. They would run their hands up the fish's body and take hold of its gills. Then they would toss it onto the riverbank. They dried and saved as much fish as they could to eat during the winter months. They also traded dried fish with other American Indians and Euro-Americans.

Wild plants were another important food. The Plateau Indians gathered camas flowers and ate their bulbs. They also dug for

Plateau Indians often hunted birds. But hunters who were very skilled might hunt bears as well.

bitterroot, wild carrots, and wild onions. They cooked these vegetables over hot stones in a pit in the ground. This was called an earth oven. They also gathered huckleberries, blueberries, and blackberries.

The Plateau Indians hunted too. They used spears and arrows to hunt small game such as wild waterfowl, quail, pheasant, geese, and duck. They also ate the eggs of these birds. Some hunters who had more strength and skills hunted bears and mountain sheep. The nations that had horses, such as the Kootenai and the Nez Perce, rode into the Plains to hunt bison.

Homes

In the winter, most Plateau Indians lived in homes that were partly underground. These homes were sometimes called pit houses. People came in and out of the house using a ladder that went through a hole in the center of the roof. This hole also let smoke from the fire inside escape. Each of the pit houses was home to one or more families. The homes were made sturdy and warm with coverings of bark or mats woven from tule (a reed that grows in marshy areas). The roofs were made from tule mats and branches. The Coeur d'Alene lived in similar houses, but theirs were not underground.

In the summer, the Plateau Indians left their villages. They moved to camps for hunting and fishing. In the camps, they built temporary shelters called lean-tos or cone-shaped lodges known as tipis. Both were made from tule mats that covered a wooden frame. The lean-tos were built to lean against a solid frame. But the tipis stood on their own. Some of the nations

This painted tipi is on display at the Flathead Indian Reservation in Montana.

HOMES BUILT BY PLATEAU INDIANS

NATION	TYPE OF HOME
Nez Perce	Double lean-to
Coeur d'Alene	Aboveground tule lodge
Klamath and Modoc	Pit houses; mat lodges; and small, rounded shelters made from grass and brush, called wickiups
Flathead	Cone-shaped lodges covered with branches or grass mats

made large double lean-tos that could house two families. The families shared one fire in the middle. Later, the Plains Indians showed Plateau peoples how to build tipis from leather. Some Plateau peoples followed this practice since the leather could easily be carried with them when they traveled.

Clothing

Plateau men usually wore only a breechcloth. These had a flap in front and a flap in back. They were held in place by a belt at the waist. They were first made of bark. Later, the Plateau Indians made the breechcloths from buckskin. When the weather grew colder, men also wore deerskin moccasins with the fur on the inside. The moccasins were often decorated with porcupine quills. Plateau Indians wore robes made from rabbit skin, bison skin, or buckskin too.

Sometimes men wore leggings made from deerskin. These leggings had a fringe along the edges and large buckskin flaps at the sides. Some men also wore shirts made from deerskin. These shirts were like a short poncho. Later, they made longer shirts with sleeves. The shirts had long fringes at the shoulders. Wealthy men wore buckskin capes too. Some were painted red, yellow, and white with images from the man's dreams.

Plateau Indians often made clothing from animal skins and decorated it with paint, quills, or beads. These Flathead and Kootenai items are decorated with beaded designs.

By about 1875, men began to dress more like Europeans. They wore pants and cotton shirts. Sometimes they wore beaded vests, neck scarves, and hats with flat brims. They usually wore their hair long and loose or in braids. Sometimes they wrapped their braids with otter fur.

Women usually wore wraparound skirts and poncho-like tops. In the early nineteenth century, they began wearing ankle-length dresses. These were made from elk, deer, and mountain-goat skin. The sides were usually left open on top, down to about the waist. They decorated the fronts of the dresses with quills or beads. Women also made woolen or

Many Plateau Indian women wore woven basket hats. These hats, like this one of Nez Perce origin, were made from bark or other plants.

TRADING FOR CLOTH

The Plateau Indians knew how to make homes and clothing from reeds and bark. But after they began trading with Euro-Americans, they used other materials, such as canvas. It was sturdy, quick, and easy to use. The Plateau peoples traded for wool too. A wool mill in Pendleton, Oregon, made Pendleton blankets. These blankets were warm and woven with bright designs. Plateau peoples wore these blankets as robes. The blankets are still very popular. Another kind of woolen cloth, called stroud, was often dyed blue or red and had a white stripe around the edge. Women used this rough cloth to make their dresses.

cotton T-shaped dresses. Women often wore cotton shirts under them. They decorated the woolen dresses with colored ribbons and placed a leather belt or sash at the waist. Women living near the Columbia River made their skirts from bark.

Like the men, women wore deerskin moccasins decorated with quills. They wore robes made from rabbit skin, bison, or buckskin. Their hair was long and loose or braided. Sometimes they wore woven basket hats. The Modoc women were known for their woven skullcap basket hats.

CHAPTER 2
SOCIETY AND CEREMONY

The nations of the Plateau were friendly with one another. They visited, fished, and gathered food together; traded goods; and often spoke one another's languages. Sometimes members of different nations would marry each other.

The Plateau Indians lived in family groups. Sometimes relatives such as grandparents, uncles, or aunts also lived with the family. Marriage was informal. Families often arranged marriages for their children. Sometimes the two families would give each other gifts to make the marriage official. Newlywed couples usually lived near the man's family. If the couple divorced, the wife would return to live with her family.

Age Rituals

Rituals were very important to the people of the Plateau nations. One important ritual was the naming ceremony. This usually happened when the child was between six months and two years of age. Parents often waited to name a child because many infants died soon after birth. But Kootenai parents named their babies at birth. Sometimes elders in the community helped choose a child's name. Children were often named after relatives. It was thought that the child would have the same characteristics as that relative.

As they neared adolescence, Plateau Indian boys and girls went on vision quests. On these quests, they would spend one or more days alone on a mountain without food. The child prayed and tried to communicate with a spirit guardian. During the vision quest, the child hoped to receive a sign from the spirit. This sign could come from a vision or some part of nature. The child would then interpret this sign to understand how to live and be successful as an adult.

ORIGINS OF CHILDREN'S NAMES

NATION	WHERE A CHILD'S NAME CAME FROM
Flathead	A dream or vision from a guardian spirit
Kootenai	Reflected the accomplishments of a relative
Nez Perce	An important ancestor

Famous Nez Perce leader Chief Joseph in ceremonial clothing

Leadership

Plateau nations were usually organized into villages or bands of extended families or of a few different families. Most of them had a chief. This chief often came from a long family line of chiefs. In some villages or bands, the chief didn't have official authority. Instead, people followed him because they believed he was a good and successful person. The chief and his family were supposed to model good behavior.

Some of the nations had more complicated leadership structures. They had a chief, a subchief, and an assembly. Every adult member, except for young unmarried men, could vote in the assembly. The Flathead had a powerful head chief who ruled over the chiefs of all the bands. He made his own decisions about going to war or making peace.

Spirituality

The Plateau Indians believed that people, animals, and trees had spirits. So did mountains, rivers, and even the sun and rain. A spiritual leader communicated between the visible world and the world of the unseen spirits. Both men and women could be spiritual leaders in the community. But it was considered more appropriate for men to take on this important role.

Storytelling was a big part of Plateau Indian life. Stories were especially important in the winter when people were home for long periods. The Plateau Indians believed their spiritual powers were stronger during the summer. This was because they were so close to nature. People often suffered from spirit sickness in the winter. Stories helped them to feel better. A story could begin one evening and last many evenings. The stories often had messages about how to be a better person. Children would also learn about their nation's history and customs from these stories.

The Plateau peoples believed that the creator of the world was Coyote. He came to the Plateau region before the people. He got rid of evil and prepared the land for them. Coyote had sacred powers that allowed him to protect his people and find food for them. One story says that Coyote came up the Columbia River and broke a dam that was keeping the salmon from swimming upstream. Coyote was not only a creator. He was a trickster who played jokes on people and animals too. The stories about the jokes he played helped people understand right and wrong behavior.

The Plateau peoples also took part in religious ceremonies. In the firstling ceremonies, the Plateau Indians honored their important foods each season. When the salmon came each spring, the people sliced the first fish into many small pieces. Everyone was given a piece to eat. They then prayed and gave thanks for the fish. The carcass was put back in the water. The people believed that this ceremony made sure that many salmon would come the next year. Some nations had similar ceremonies when the first berries of the season were ripe.

When winter arrived, almost all the Plateau nations held a winter spirit dance. The people gave thanks for the past year. They asked for protection and success for the coming year. Some of the nations, such as the Flathead, Kootenai, and Pend d'Oreille, called their ceremony the Jump Dance.

Medicine

Plateau Indian healers had several methods for healing both spiritual and physical illnesses. Sometimes they made teas and medicines from herbs. They might perform rituals using plants, animals, and small figures believed to have magical powers too.

The sweat lodge was an important part of healing for the Plateau Indians. Here, people were cured of sicknesses in the body and spirit. They also gained skills and strength for tasks

Sweat lodges, such as this structure built by the Nez Perce, were an important part of healing for Plateau Indians.

such as fishing and hunting. Some sweat lodges were built to fit just two people. Others could hold more than ten. The dome-shaped lodges were covered with animal skins or blankets and had a small flap for an entryway. A small pit was in the center of each one. Stones were heated in a fire outside of the sweat lodge and then put into the pit and sprinkled with water. This made steam, which caused the people inside to sweat. As they sweated, they sang or chanted prayers.

Sometimes many people took part in healing ceremonies. The people would gather around, singing and beating drums or sticks. The healer might recite a charm or give the sick person medicine. The healer sometimes massaged the sick person or leaned over the person to suck the sickness from the body. Some healers put their mouths directly over the affected part of the body. Nez Perce healers used a bone whistle or a small funnel made from a leaf to suck out the illness.

A Nez Perce bone whistle

CHAPTER 3
FUNCTIONAL ART

A Salish woven bag made from natural fibers and colored yarn

Like many American Indians, the Plateau Indians made art that was useful. Art was part of their everyday lives. They wove baskets, bags, mats, and blankets. They decorated these items with woven designs, beads, and quills. They made jewelry. And they depicted their lives through paintings and carvings.

Weaving
Plateau Indians were famous for their weaving. They often carried bags known as cornhusk bags. These flat bags were made using grass

Cornhusk bags were common among Plateau Indians. These Nez Perce bags are made from grasses and colorful yarn.

and other plant materials. Later, twine or wool might be used. Cornhusks were another strong material that was used to weave and decorate the bags. The bags were woven tightly and without seams. They also had colorful geometric designs. Usually the design on the front was different from the one on the back. Sometimes the designs were woven so that they could be seen on the outside of the bag, but not on the inside.

These bags had many uses. They held roots, berries, fish, or personal belongings. Sometimes the bags were worn around the hip. They might also be used as saddle bags. Later, smaller bags became common. These might be made of leather and wool and decorated with beads. The beading could be very complex, showing pictures of animals or patterns with flowers. Often these bags were given as gifts. They were known as friendship bags.

Plateau Indians also wove baskets of many sizes and shapes from grasses, birch bark, spruce, or cedar. They decorated the baskets with patterns or pictures of animals. One common pattern made the baskets look like they were decorated with square tiles. The simplest baskets were used for storing dry food or gathering berries. These were known as cylinder bags, or Sally bags. Sometimes the Plateau peoples rubbed sticky sap from pine trees on the inside. This made the basket waterproof. They also made baskets for cooking hot foods such as soup or stew. A cooking basket was woven around a flat rock. To cook in it, a woman heated smaller rocks in a fire and dropped them into the basket. The heat cooked food on top of the rocks.

This Flathead beaded purse has a blue background, which was common in Plateau beadwork.

Beads, Quills, and Jewelry

Clothing, moccasins, and bags were often decorated with beads. Beads were made from shells, bones, pebbles, claws, nuts, seeds, horns, pieces of metal, and bird talons. Porcupine quills were used for decoration too. The quills were flattened and dyed using berries or plants. Quills were then sewn onto leather

A RISE IN BEADWORK

The native peoples of the Plateau decorated their clothing and belongings with pieces of shells, bones, teeth, and quills. But through trade with Euro-Americans and other American Indian nations, they got glass beads. These beads were made in Italy, China, and Czechoslovakia (a former country made up of present-day Slovakia and the Czech Republic).

This trade began in the early nineteenth century, around the time explorers Meriwether Lewis and William Clark were traveling through the country. The first beads Plateau Indians got were called pony beads. These were fairly large glass beads. They were often black, white, red, or blue. Green and yellow beads were less common. The Plateau peoples sewed these beads to cloth in blocks or strips.

Later, smaller beads called seed beads became popular. These beads came in more colors and could be used to create more complex designs. Plateau Indians beaded clothing, moccasins, cradleboards, and bags with patterns and pictures. As white and blue beads were the least expensive, these colors were often used to create a background for the design.

Beadwork became a sign of wealth for the Plateau peoples. Beads and beaded objects soon became an important part of trade in the Plateau region.

This Flathead purse is beaded with a floral pattern.

The Pend d'Oreille often wore large earrings made from shells, like the ones this girl is wearing.

or cloth. But the color of the quills would fade over time. When Plateau peoples began trading, glass beads became popular. The beads stayed bright and were easier to use than other materials. Beads were valuable too. Over time, Plateau Indian beading became more and more complex. Plateau Indians beaded flowers, animals, people, and even scenes from stories. They would also fill an entire surface with beads of one color, to give the scene a background.

For jewelry, Plateau Indians made necklaces of copper tubes, shells, and bones. Sometimes their necklaces had up to fourteen strands. They made earrings too. Many of the Pend d'Oreille wore large shell earrings that dangled from their ears.

Images of People and Animals

Plateau Indians painted animals, humans, and spiritual figures on large rocks and cliffs. These rock paintings were most common among the Kootenai and other nations that lived in what is now British Columbia. They mixed red ocher with oil or fish eggs to make paint. The paintings may have been created

Plateau Indians created rock paintings throughout the region. These paintings may have been used for religious purposes or to tell stories.

for religious ceremonies. Some seem to be connected to vision quests or communication with spirits. But the paintings may also have been part of a hunting ritual or used to tell stories or give messages to one another. The sites where these paintings can be seen are considered sacred by Plateau Indians. Many of these paintings can still be seen in the Plateau region.

CHAPTER 4
FACING CHANGE

Plateau Indian life changed after the Great Basin Indians brought horses to the Plateau region in about **1700.** Then the Plateau Indians could travel into the Plains to hunt buffalo. They also met many Plains Indians. So the Plateau peoples began using Plains techniques to make their homes and clothing.

Once horses became part of the Plateau Indian culture, the Cayuse, the Nez Perce, and the Palouse became known for breeding the animals. Being able to travel by horseback let the Plateau Indians trade more. They could travel farther and carry more on their horses than they could with canoes. And they were able to trade the horses they bred for goods such as blankets, buffalo robes, paint, and even gold coins.

At the beginning of the nineteenth century, Euro-American explorers and traders began moving west and into the Plateau Indians' land. In 1805 and 1806, Lewis and Clark met Plateau Indians. The first peoples they met were the Nez Perce. This nation was friendly. They gave Lewis and Clark food, canoes, and shelter. Soon after, Euro-American and American Indian fur traders came to the region.

In 1820, a group of Iroquois (EER-uh-kwah) fur traders came to Montana from the Northeast. These Iroquois had been educated by priests in a Catholic mission. The Iroquois leader, Old Ignace, began to teach Catholicism to the Plateau peoples. They welcomed his teachings. Catholic prayers and rituals became a part of the religious life of those Plateau Indians. They even asked for more Christian missionaries and priests to come to them. From 1820 until about 1850, Christian missionaries had a strong presence among the Plateau Indians.

By the 1840s, thousands of Euro-Americans were traveling through the Columbia Plateau on their way farther west. They often traveled on Plateau nation lands. This led to conflicts between them and the Plateau peoples. The Euro-Americans also brought diseases such as measles to the Plateau Indians.

For many years, Christian missionaries lived among the Plateau Indians. They taught religion and set up missions, such as the Saint Mary's Mission, shown here.

PIERRE-JEAN DE SMET

Pierre-Jean De Smet

Pierre-Jean De Smet was a Jesuit priest who ministered to American Indians across the United States. He first lived and worked with the Potawatomi Indians in Iowa. In 1840, he heard that the Flathead were looking for a priest, so he moved to Montana. He founded the Saint Mary's Mission in Montana in 1841. He started many more missions in the West. All the American Indians he met trusted him. He helped settle conflicts between many nations. He helped bring peace between American Indian nations and Euro-Americans too. In 1868, De Smet helped the US government agree on a peace treaty with several Plains Indian nations. He died in 1873.

These diseases spread quickly, and many Plateau peoples died. By 1850, the Plateau Indian population was half of what it had been in 1800. The US government tried to make treaties with the Plateau nations. The government wanted to ease the conflicts by dividing the land between the government and the Plateau Indians. But in 1857, gold was discovered in the region. Miners and Euro-Americans came there. This led to more conflicts.

The presence of Euro-Americans disrupted the Plateau way of life. Euro-American mining and fishing left fewer salmon for Plateau peoples. Both the US and the Canadian governments began to force the Plateau nations to accept Euro-American culture. The governments took over Plateau Indian land. The native peoples were placed on reservations. Some nations were forced to give up all their land. They had to move to reservations in other parts of the country.

On reservations, they had to give up fishing and hunting. Instead, they farmed. Their children were sent to boarding schools where they were not allowed to speak their native languages. They had to wear Euro-American clothing and hairstyles. They could not keep anything they had brought from home. In 1876, the Canadian government passed the Indian Act. This act encouraged the Plateau peoples to give up their rights as native peoples and become Canadian citizens. The act said

Many Euro-Americans moved to the Plateau region after gold was discovered there. They set up camps and cities, like this one in Montana.

that if Plateau Indians learned to read and signed a pledge to "live as a white," they would be allowed to vote and own property. Very few chose to do so.

WARS BETWEEN THE US GOVERNMENT AND PLATEAU PEOPLES

NATION	YEAR	PLATEAU NATION LEADER	REASON FOR WAR
Cayuse	1847–1850	Chief Tiloukaikt	Cayuse children died from measles in a Christian mission.
Yakama, Cayuse, and Walla Walla	1855–1858	Chief Kamiakin (Yakama)	Miners trespassed on Yakama land.
Coeur d'Alene, Palouse, and Spokane	1858	Chief Vincent (Coeur d'Alene)	Euro-Americans disobeyed the land treaty.
Modoc	1872–1873	Kintpuash (Captain Jack)	The government moved the Modoc to the Klamath reservation.
Nez Perce	1877	Chief Joseph	The Nez Perce refused to move onto the reservation and tried to flee to Canada.

The destruction of their traditional lifestyle caused many wars between the Plateau nations and the US and Canadian governments. The Modoc Nation had been moved from its land in California onto a Klamath reservation in Oregon. In 1870, they tried to go back to California. This led to the Modoc War. The war lasted one year, and the Modoc lost. In 1877, a band of Nez Perce tried to flee to Canada instead of moving onto a reservation. US armies chased them for 1,700 miles (2,736 kilometers) over mountains and rivers. They fought many battles. The Nez Perce chief finally surrendered just 30 miles (48 km) from the Canadian border. This war is one of the most famous in the history of the American Indians' struggle against the US government.

The US government continued to take lands away from Plateau nations well into the twentieth century. In 1887, the government tried to stop Plateau Indians from sharing land and resources. They divided reservations and gave small plots of land to individual families. The rest of the land was sold. The Plateau nations lost a lot of their land. They could no longer hunt. They struggled to find enough food and other materials to live.

CHAPTER 5

A THRIVING LAND AND CULTURE

By the end of the nineteenth century, many Plateau peoples lived on reservations. Government workers controlled the lives of people there. American Indians were forced to give up their identities and traditions.

Fighting for Rights and Land

In 1934, the US government passed the Indian Reorganization Act (IRA). Its goal was to make life better for American Indians on reservations. They were allowed to share land and resources again. Nations could own their reservations and create tribal councils to govern them. Members of the councils were elected by the nation. The US government would help train American Indian youth for work and provide health care and other services to American Indian nations.

In 1954, the US government believed that some nations had become wealthy enough that they no longer needed government help. The government introduced termination. Under this policy, some American Indian nations would no longer receive aid from the government. Instead, these nations would be part of American society. The government took control of American Indian land and no longer recognized individual nations. The Klamath was one of the nations that was terminated. Their lands were filled with trees and other natural resources that the government sold. When the Klamath lost their land, they did not have the resources to develop and thrive in American society. The Klamath and other nations sued the government to win back their American Indian status. In August 1986, they finally succeeded.

In the second half of the twentieth century, many other Plateau nations also sued the US and Canadian governments. They claimed that their lands had been stolen or bought for less than they were worth. They also said that they could no longer fish in their rivers because dams had chased away the fish. They wanted to be paid back for the loss of their land and fishing sites. Most nations received money for both losses.

Throughout the late twentieth and early twenty-first centuries, many Plateau nations worked hard to build a strong economy and to revive their land and rivers. The people began working in timber, ranching, and fishing industries. They also built tourist resorts and casinos. The Coeur d'Alene Nation runs the Coeur d'Alene Casino in Idaho. They also have a medical center and a tribal school. The Kootenai Tribe of Idaho runs the Kootenai River Inn Casino and Spa and the Twin Rivers Canyon Resort.

Caring for the Environment

Many of the Plateau nations see themselves as caretakers of the environment. Some that operate resorts and casinos work to fix environmental problems in their regions too. The Kootenai have established the Kootenai Valley Resource Initiative to protect natural resources and Plateau Indian culture. The Yakama, Umatilla, Warm Springs, and Nez Perce tribes formed the Columbia River Inter-Tribal Fish Commission (CRITFC) in 1977. This organization works to protect salmon and the tribal fishing rights along the river.

About 78 percent of American Indians no longer live on reservations. But the Plateau Indian nations have several large reservation populations. Most of the Flathead live on the Flathead Indian Reservation in Montana. The formal name of this reservation is the Confederated Salish and Kootenai Tribes of the Flathead Reservations. The Cayuse, Umatilla, and Walla

American Indians from many nations live on or near the Flathead Indian Reservation in Montana, shown here.

Walla live on the Confederated Tribes of the Umatilla Indian Reservation. Nearly fifteen hundred members live on or near this reservation. Many still practice a religion called Washat and speak their native languages. They teach the language to the younger generation too. Their community school has a language program for children aged three to five. They also offer language classes to older children and members of the community.

Museums and cultural organizations help preserve the cultural heritage of the Plateau Indians and share it with others. The Yakama Nation Museum in Toppenish, Washington, opened in 1980. It is one of the oldest American Indian museums in the United States. An exhibit at the High Desert Museum of Bend,

The Yakama Nation Cultural Center houses one of the oldest American Indian museums in the United States.

A representation of Cayuse Indian culture at the Tamástslikt Cultural Institute

Oregon, shows how the Plateau Indians changed from living in traditional ways to becoming active members of modern American society. The Tamástslikt Cultural Institute in Pendleton, Oregon, celebrates both the past and the present lives of the Cayuse, Umatilla, and Walla Walla.

Like many other American Indians, the Plateau Indians work to develop and protect what has always been most important to them. This includes their land, their languages, their cultures, and their faith. And whether they live on reservations or among other American citizens, they seek balance between their lives as Americans and American Indians.

PLATEAU POPULATIONS

NATION	POPULATION
Yakama	11,527
Nez Perce	6,705
Modoc	1,732
Klamath	4,413
Kootenai	1,130
Flathead	7,673
Okanagan	1,985
Shuswap	263
Chilcotin	3,000

* Numbers according to 2010 US Census and 2016 Canadian data

NOTABLE PLATEAU INDIANS

Sherman Alexie (Coeur d'Alene/Spokane)
wrote *The Absolutely True Diary of a Part-Time Indian*, which won the National Book Award for Young People's Literature in 2007. He has published many works of poetry, short stories, and novels. He also cowrote the screenplay for the award-winning 1998 film *Smoke Signals*. This movie was based on his short story "This Is What It Means to Say Phoenix, Arizona."

N. Kathryn Brigham (Umatilla)
was one of the founders of the Columbia River Inter-Tribal Fish Commission in 1977. One of the CRITFC's main goals is to protect the rights of native peoples to fish in the Columbia River. They also want to make sure that the fishing supply is available for many generations to come.

Hattie Kauffman (Nez Perce)
was the first American Indian to file a news story on a national television evening broadcast. She has worked for ABC and CBS and has won four Emmy Awards for her work. She wrote a memoir, *Falling into Place: A Memoir of Overcoming*, in 2012.

Shoni Schimmel (Umatilla)
plays basketball for the Atlanta Dream of the Women's National Basketball Association (WNBA). She was selected as the 2014 WNBA All-Star Game Most Valuable Player. She has also played basketball for the University of Louisville and for Team USA in the 2013 World University Games in Russia, where her team won a gold medal.

Timeline

Each Plateau Indian culture had its own way of recording history. This timeline is based on the Gregorian calendar, which Europeans brought to North America.

Ca. 1700   Native peoples from other cultures introduce horses to the Plateau region.

1805   The Nez Perce and Yakama both encounter the expedition led by explorers Meriwether Lewis and William Clark.

1820   A group of Catholic-educated Iroquois Indians arrives in Montana and teaches Catholicism to Plateau peoples.

1840s   Euro-Americans travel through the Plateau on their way west, disrupting the lives of the Plateau Indians by trespassing and spreading disease. The Plateau Indian population is dramatically reduced.

1847   The Cayuse War begins.

1855   The three-year Yakama War begins.

1857   Gold is discovered on several rivers in the Plateau, further disrupting the lives of Plateau nations.

1858   The Coeur d'Alene War is fought.

1872   The Modoc War begins.

1876   The Canadian government passes the Indian Act.

1877   The Nez Perce War is fought.

1934   The Indian Reorganization Act establishes self-government for American Indian nations.

1954   The US government begins its policy of termination. Modoc and Klamath nations sue for the return of their federal status with the US government.

1977   The Nez Perce, Yakama, Umatilla, and Warm Springs form the CRITFC.

1986   The Modoc and Klamath nations win their suit against the US government.

2015   The Kootenai Valley Resource Initiative launches the Bonners Ferry Islands project to restore the population of sturgeon in the Kootenai River.

Glossary

canvas: a strong, rough cloth that is used to make tents, sails, and bags

carcass: the body of a dead animal

ceremony: a spiritual celebration or event

citizen: a person who legally belongs to a country and has rights and protection there

Euro-American: someone living in the United States who is of European descent

harpoon: a long weapon, often used for hunting whales or large animals

Jesuit: relating to a religious group called the Roman Catholic Society of Jesus

language family: a group of similar languages

mission: a place where a group of foreign people do religious work

nation: an independent group of people with a shared history, culture, and governing system

ocher: an earthy, impure iron ore used to make color, as in paint

preserve: to keep something in its original condition

reservation: an area of land set aside by the US government for an American Indian nation

revive: to make something strong and active again

treaty: an official agreement

Selected Bibliography

Chesney Cowles Memorial Museum. *Cornhusk Bags of the Plateau Indians*. Chicago: University of Chicago Press, 1976.

Josephy, Alvin M., Jr. *The Nez Perce Indians and the Opening of the Northwest*. New York: Houghton Mifflin, 1997.

Keyser, James D. *Indian Rock Art of the Columbia Plateau*. Seattle: University of Washington Press, 1992.

Moulton, Candy. *Everyday Life among the American Indians: 1800–1900*. Cincinnati: Writer's Digest Books, 2001.

Reader's Digest Association. *Through Indian Eyes: The Untold Story of Native American Peoples*. Pleasantville, NY: Reader's Digest Association, 1995.

Further Information

Campbell, Nicola I. *Shin-chi's Canoe.* Toronto: Groundwood Books, 2008. Even older readers will enjoy this artful picture-book story of a young boy who tries to hold onto his traditions after being sent to a residential school.

Canada's First Peoples
http://firstpeoplesofcanada.com/index.html
This website explores the cultures of the American Indians who lived in the part of North America that is now Canada, including the Plateau Indians.

Expand learning beyond the printed book. Download free, complementary educational resources for this book from our website, www.lernerresource.com.

Columbia River Inter-Tribal Fish Commission
http://www.critfc.org/for-kids-home/for-kids/indians-and-indian-tribes
This website is maintained by the Yakama, Umatilla, Warm Springs, and Nez Perce tribes, which are linked by their dependence on salmon. Explore more about these four tribes.

Confederated Tribes of the Umatilla Indian Reservation
http://ctuir.org/history-culture
Read all about the history, culture, and language of the Umatilla, Cayuse, and Walla Walla nations.

Gimpel, Diane Marczely. *A Timeline History of Early American Indian Peoples*. Minneapolis: Lerner Publications, 2015. Learn basic historical facts and important historical dates for five major groups of early Americans, including the Plateau nations.

Goddu, Krystyna Poray. *Native Peoples of the Great Basin*. Minneapolis: Lerner Publications, 2017. Learn about the culture and history of the Plateau Indians' closest neighbors.

The Klamath Tribes
http://klamathtribes.org/history
Visit this website to learn more about the Klamath and Modoc.

Montana Kids
http://montanakids.com/history_and_prehistory/indian_reservations/flathead.htm
This website includes a section on the Flathead Indian Reservation, home to the Confederated Salish and Kootenai nations.

Nez Perce
http://www.nezperce.org/Official/history.htm
Go to the official website of the Nez Perce to learn about their history and read frequently asked questions about the nation.

Index

art, 24–29

chief, 20, 35
Christianity, 31, 34
clothing, 8, 14–17, 26–27, 30, 33
Columbia River, 5, 10, 17, 21, 38
Coyote, 5, 21–22

dance, 22
De Smet, Pierre-Jean, 32

environment, 37–38
Euro-American, 8–9, 11, 17, 27, 30–34

firstling ceremony, 22
fishing, 10–13, 18, 22, 32–33, 37–38

government, 9, 32–37
Great Basin Indians, 7, 30

healer, 22–23
homes, 13–14, 17, 30
horses, 13, 30
hunting, 10, 12–13, 22, 29–30, 33, 35

Iroquois, 31

language family, 7
leather, 8, 14, 17, 25–26
Lewis and Clark, 27, 30

marriage, 18
museum, 39

names, 18–19, 38

Old Ignace, 31

pit house, 13–14
Plains Indians, 7–8, 13–14, 30, 32
plateau, 5–15, 17–22, 24–41

religion, 22, 29, 31, 39
reservation, 9, 33–36, 38–40

salmon, 10–11, 21–22, 32, 38
storytelling, 21
sweat lodge, 22–23

termination, 37
tipi, 13–14

vision quest, 19, 29

war, 20, 34–35
weaving, 13, 24–26

Photo Acknowledgments

The images in this book are used with the permission of: © iStockphoto.com/Bastar (paper background); © lienkie/123RF.com (tanned hide background); © Dennis Frates/Alamy, pp. 2–3; © Laura Westlund/Independent Picture Service, pp. 4, 6; © Michael Wheatley/All Canada Photos/Getty Images, p. 8; Library of Congress, pp. 9 (LC-USZ62-46997), 28 (LC-USZ62-113092), 32 (LC-DIG-cwpbh-03561); © Tom Murphy/National Geographic/Getty Images, p. 10; © Marilyn Angel Wynn/Nativestock.com, pp. 11, 13, 15, 16, 20, 23, 24, 25, 26, 27; © iStockphoto.com/mikewweston, p. 12; © Danita Delimont/Gallo Images/Getty Images, p. 29; The Denver Public Library, Western History Collection, Source: P. J. De Smet, "Oregon Missions and Travels over the Rocky Mountains in 1845–1846." New York: 1847, Call # X-31114, p. 31; The Granger Collection, New York, p. 33; © Andre Jenny/Alamy, p. 38; © George Ostertag/Alamy, p. 39; © WorldFoto/Alamy, p. 40.

Front cover: © iStockphoto.com/fisfra.

J 970.4 GOD

Goddu, Krystyna Poray,

Native peoples of the Plateau

JUN 1 5 2017